THE DOG BOOK

by

JAN PFLOOG

Dandie Dinmont Terrier

A GOLDEN BOOK • NEW YORK
WESTERN PUBLISHING COMPANY, INC., RACINE, WISCONSIN 53404

Some dogs are
very, very BIG.

Saint Bernard

Other dogs are
middle-sized...

Golden Retriever

**and some are
very, very** LITTLE.

Chihuahua

Some dogs have very short legs.

Dachshund

Some dogs have
very long legs.

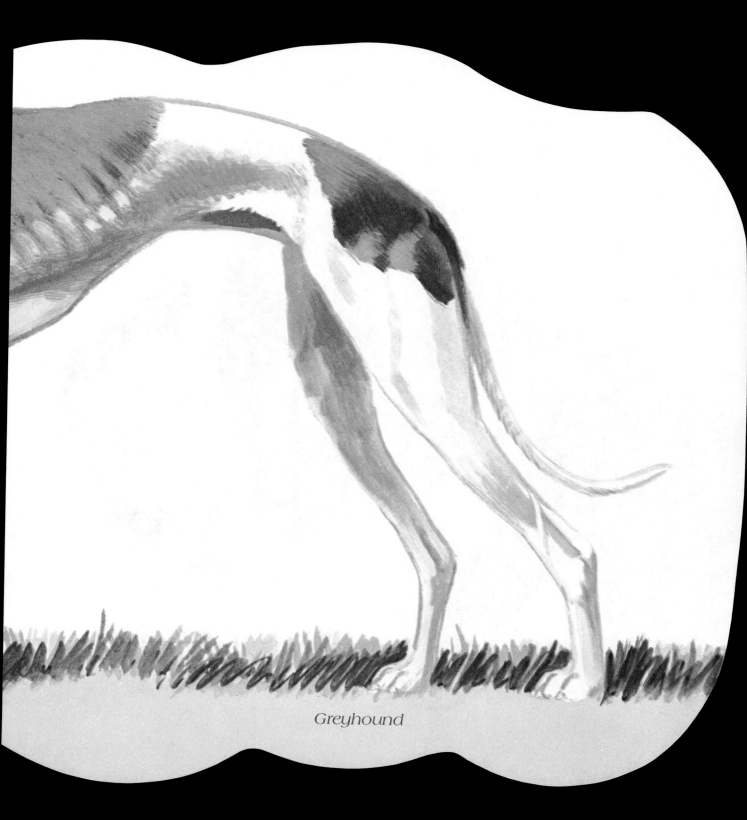

Greyhound

Some dogs have a short, snubby nose.

Bulldog

Others have a long,
pointy nose.

Russian Wolfhound

Some dogs have long, shaggy hair.

Skye Terrier

Some dogs have
short, smooth hair.

Pointer

Some dogs have long,
silky ears that hang down...

Basset Hound

and others have short,
sharp ears that stick up.

Cairn Terrier

Poodle

Some dogs have
a fancy coat.

Dalmatian

Some dogs have a plain coat.

Labrador Retriever

Some dogs have a BIG
curly tail, and others . . .

Eskimo Dog

have a LITTLE
curly tail.

Pug

And some dogs have almost *no* tail at all!

Boston Terrier

What kind of dog is your favorite?